6 August 1945

August 6, 1945

The
Bombing
of
Hiroshima

John Malam

Smart Apple Media

First published by Cherrytree Press
(a member of the Evans Publishing Group)
327 High Street, Slough
Berkshire SL1 1TX, United Kingdom
Copyright © 2002 Evans Brothers Limited
This edition published under license from
Evans Brothers Limited. All rights reserved.

Designed by Neil Sayer, Edited by Louise John

Published in the United States by
Smart Apple Media
1980 Lookout Drive
North Mankato, MN 56003

U.S. publication copyright © 2003 Smart Apple Media
International copyright reserved in all countries. No part of this book may be
reproduced in any form without written permission from the publisher.
Printed in Hong Kong

Library of Congress Cataloging-in-Publication Data

Malam, John, 1957- The bombing of Hiroshima / by John Malam.
p. cm. — (Dates with history) Includes index. Summary: Relates how
scientists in several countries over a period of many years conducted research
that ultimately led to the invention of the atomic bomb, which was then used
against Japan in the hope of ending World War II. Contents: The search for a
super-bomb — Splitting the atom — America enters the war — The
Manhattan Project — Testing the atomic bomb — An important meeting —
A secret plan — The target cities — Hiroshima is bombed — Death of a city
and its people — Nagasaki is bombed.
ISBN 1-58340-213-6
1. Hiroshima-shi (Japan)—History—Bombardment, 1945—Juvenile literature.
2. Atomic bomb—Juvenile literature. 3. World War, 1939-1945—Japan—
Hiroshima-shi—Juvenile literature. 4. World War, 1939-1945—Japan—
Juvenile literature. [1. Hiroshima-shi (Japan)—History—Bombardment, 1945.
2. Atomic bomb. 3. World War, 1939-1945—Japan—Hiroshima-shi.]
I. Title. II. Series.

D767.25.H6 M25 2002   940.54'25—dc21   2002023101

9 8 7 6 5 4 3 2 1

Picture credits:
Corbis: 11, 16, 17, 23
Hulton Getty: 8, 20
Science Museum / Science & Society Picture Library: 6, 7, 9
Science Photo Library: 12, 13, 14, 22
Topham Picturepoint: Front cover, 10, 15, 18, 19, 24, 25, 26, 29

Contents

The Search for a Superbomb

The story of how the world's most terrible weapon was invented began many years before it was used in the Second World War in 1945. In 1896, the French scientist Henri Becquerel discovered that atoms—the tiny particles of solid matter from which everything is made—give off energy.

The world's scientists were fascinated by Becquerel's discovery, and they soon realized that atoms contained huge amounts of stored-up energy. In 1904, a British scientist, Frederick Soddy, wondered if energy from

Much of the early work on splitting the atom would have been done in a science laboratory similar to this one.

atoms could be used to make a weapon. So scientists in Europe and Scandinavia began the search to find a way to "**split the atom**." Whoever succeeded would know how to force atoms to release their energy: they would have the secret for making an **atomic bomb**.

In August 1939, **Albert Einstein**, one of the world's most brilliant scientists, wrote to the president of the United States, **Franklin D. Roosevelt**. Einstein said:

World-famous scientist Albert Einstein, talking about his ideas in 1935.

> "Sir . . . the element **uranium** may be turned into a new and important source of energy in the immediate future. . . . This new phenomenon would also lead to the construction of bombs, and it is conceivable that extremely powerful bombs of a new type may thus be constructed."

One month after Einstein wrote to the president, the Second World War began. It ended six years later, in August 1945, when two bombs destroyed the Japanese cities of Hiroshima and Nagasaki. The bombs were atomic bombs, the deadliest weapon ever invented.

Splitting the Atom

The 1930s were a time of great change in Germany because the Nazi Party, led by Adolf Hitler, had come to power. Under the Nazis, certain groups of people in Germany were persecuted, especially the Jewish community, many of whom sought refuge in the United States.

Among the Jews who fled from Nazi Germany were many scientists. They knew that German scientists were experimenting with a substance called uranium, and they

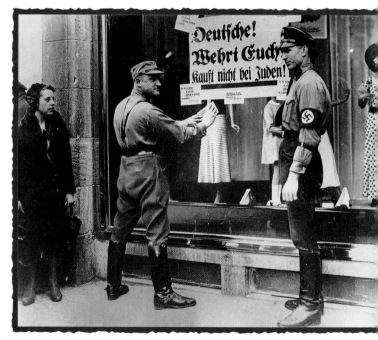

Nazi soldiers place notices on Jewish stores, urging German people not to buy Jewish goods.

feared that Germany was very close to building an atomic bomb.

In 1938, scientists in Germany did succeed in splitting the atom of uranium, a silvery-white metallic element. They figured out that if uranium atoms could be split over and over again, in a **chain reaction** over a very short period of time, the result would be a massive atomic explosion.

Leo Szilard reads a newspaper warning that the Russians might have made an atomic bomb.

On September 1, 1939, the German army invaded Poland. Two days later, on September 3, Britain and France declared war on Germany, and the Second World War began.

One month before the start of the war, three of the scientists who had fled to the United States—Leo Szilard, Eugene Wigner, and Edward Teller—told Albert Einstein to write his letter to President Roosevelt. Einstein had also fled Nazi Germany, and because he was world-famous the scientists hoped the president would be interested in what he had to say. He was.

America Enters the War

Even though the United States was at peace in 1939, President Roosevelt instructed his officials to look into Einstein's suggestions.

At first, the war was a war between the powers of Europe and there seemed to be no reason for the United States to become involved. However, on October 19, 1939, President Roosevelt replied to Einstein. He wanted the U.S. to be first to develop an atomic bomb, not Germany. The letter said:

"My dear Professor,
I want to thank you for your recent letter. . . . I found this data of such import that I have convened a Board . . . to thoroughly investigate the possibilities of your suggestion regarding the element of uranium."

The American effort to build an atomic bomb got off to a slow start, mainly because the U.S. was not involved in the war and there was no urgency to develop it. This changed on December 7, 1941, when, without warning,

Japanese warplanes attacked U.S. Navy ships at their Pearl Harbor base, on the Pacific island of Hawaii. Some 2,400 American servicemen and civilians were killed.

Japan was already fighting a war with China, and to keep its army supplied it had been buying scrap metal and oil from America. In 1940, Japan declared its support for Germany. So in July 1941, the U.S. stopped sending war supplies to Japan. This angered the Japanese government, who began to plan the raid on Pearl Harbor. When the attack came, it brought the U.S. into the Second World War.

U.S. Navy ships are bombed during the attack on Pearl Harbor, Hawaii.

The Manhattan Project

At about the same time as the Pearl Harbor attack, a top-secret project began in the U.S. It was code-named the Manhattan Project, after the borough of Manhattan in New York City, where it had its first headquarters. Its aim was simple: to build an atomic bomb before the enemy did.

Work on the Manhattan Project was soon under way between the Americans and the British. There was an added urgency to their work, since both sides thought Germany was very close to building an atomic bomb. However, what no one in the U.S. or Britain knew at the time was that Germany had actually decided *not* to build an atomic bomb. German officials thought it would be too expensive—and they believed they would win the war, anyway.

In November 1942, the head of the Manhattan Project, **General Leslie R. Groves**, and the project's top scientist, **Dr. Robert Oppenheimer**, chose a site for their main laboratory at Los Alamos, a small town in the mountains of New Mexico. It was chosen because it was far away from large towns and cities, and

The high-security, top-secret laboratory at Los Alamos opened in April 1943.

there were desert areas where explosions could be set off in secret.

Building an atomic bomb required money—the project cost an estimated $2 billion, which was a lot in the 1940s. It also needed people. By 1944, around 129,000 people were working on the Manhattan Project, but only a few knew what they were building.

The Los Alamos laboratory produced two atomic bombs, each of a different type. One used uranium to produce an explosion and the other used **plutonium**—another silvery-white metallic element. The scientists gave nicknames to the bombs. The uranium bomb was named Little Boy, because of its long, thin shape. The plutonium bomb, which was much rounder, was named Fat Man.

Models of the Little Boy (left) and Fat Man (right) atomic bombs.

Testing the Atomic Bomb

America's atomic bombs were finished by the end of 1944—but would they work? In the south of New Mexico, 230 miles (370 km) from Los Alamos, was the remote Alamogordo Bombing Range, where the U.S. military tried out new weapons. It was here, in an area code-named Trinity, that the world's first atomic bomb was tested.

The Trinity Test took place at dawn on July 16, 1945, when a plutonium test bomb, nicknamed Jumbo, was detonated at the top of a 98-foot-tall (30 m) tower. It exploded with the force of 20,900 tons (19,000 t) of ordinary explosives. A flash of light brighter than any ever seen lit up the desert, and 425 scientists and technicians

The mushroom-shaped cloud of the Trinity Test explosion rose 40,206 feet (12,200 m) into the sky.

watched as a huge fireball became a mushroom-shaped cloud. The temperature at Ground Zero—the place directly underneath the bomb tower—was three times as hot as the sun, and a crater measuring 2,400 feet (730 m) across was blasted into the desert. America's atomic bomb worked. A deadly superbomb had been created.

Only after the war did Robert Oppenheimer's part in the Manhattan Project become known. This is what he said about the Trinity Test explosion:

Robert Oppenheimer (right) and General Groves stand at the remains of the tower on which the first atomic bomb was detonated.

"We waited until the blast had passed, walked out of the shelter and then it was extremely solemn. We knew the world would not be the same. A few people laughed, a few people cried. Most people were silent. I remembered the line from the Hindu scripture, the Bhagavad-Gita: 'Now I am become Death, the destroyer of worlds.' I suppose we all thought that, one way or another."

An Important Meeting

At the beginning of the Manhattan Project in 1942, Germany was the most likely future target for an atomic bomb. However, as the war progressed, the U.S. and Britain realized that Germany was not going to build its own atomic bomb. By early 1945, Germany was close to defeat. Hitler killed himself in April, and on May 8, Germany surrendered. The war in Europe was over, but the Pacific war—between America and Japan—raged on.

On July 17, 1945, the day after the Trinity Test, a conference began at Potsdam, near Berlin, the German capital. At the meeting were the leaders of the countries that had defeated Germany: the new president of the U.S

Devastation in the Japanese capital city of Tokyo caused by firebombs during the Pacific war.

From left to right, leaders Churchill, Truman, and Stalin, photographed at the Potsdam Conference, 1945.

Harry S. Truman, the British prime minister, **Winston Churchill**, and **Josef Stalin**, leader of the Soviet Union.

At the Potsdam Conference, the victorious leaders talked about the rebuilding of Europe. They were concerned with what to do about the defeated Germany and where to place borders for the countries involved in the war, particularly Poland. The main talking point, however, was how to end the Pacific war.

A Secret Plan

President Truman learned about the successful test-firing of the atomic bomb while he was at the Potsdam Conference. He was pleased that the test had gone so well. To his way of thinking the atomic bomb could be used to bring the war in the Pacific to a quick end and, therefore, save American lives. However, he had to take into account a difficult political situation.

The problem was that the Soviet Union was not at war with Japan. However, at the Potsdam Conference, Josef

Harry S. Truman became the 33rd President of the U.S. after President Roosevelt died in April 1945.

A U.S. Marine aims his machine gun at a Japanese sniper during the battle of Okinawa in the Pacific war.

Stalin agreed to join forces with the United States and Britain and go to war against Japan. The Soviet Union would declare war on Japan by August 15, and the plan was for American, British, and Soviet forces to invade Japan. But there was another plan, which the Soviet Union knew nothing about.

President Truman had something else in mind. Now that the U.S. had the atomic bomb, maybe he didn't need help from the Soviet Union after all. The fact is, the U.S. and the Soviet Union didn't really trust each other. Both wanted to become major world powers after the war, and now that the U.S. had the atomic bomb, President Truman knew he had something the Soviet Union didn't. This was the political reason why the U.S. wanted to use its new weapon—to get the "upper hand" over the Soviet Union.

The Target Cities

The city of Hiroshima in 1930, before the atomic bomb was dropped.

On July 21,1945, five days after the Trinity Test, and while President Truman was still at the Potsdam Conference, he gave the go-ahead for the atomic bomb to be used. It was to be used before August 15, which was when the Soviet Union had said they would enter the war against Japan.

Before the Potsdam Conference ended, Japan was given a chance to surrender. Japan refused. The conference ended on August 2, and the events that took place over the following seven days were to change the course of history. While plans for the invasion of Japan were going ahead, secret preparations had already been made to use the atomic bomb.

U.S. military leaders decided that the atomic bomb should be dropped in broad daylight, and only if the weather was good. Also, it should be used against a city that had not already been damaged by **conventional bombs**. This way the full force of an atomic explosion would be seen, and Japan would be so shocked it would surrender.

Four Japanese cities were chosen as targets. They were, in this order: Kyoto, Hiroshima, Kokura, and Niigata. Objections were raised about bombing Kyoto, an ancient city of great religious importance to the Japanese, so it was removed from the list. Kyoto was spared, and Hiroshima became first choice. The city of Nagasaki was added instead, in fourth place on the list. Instructions were issued to the U.S. Air Force not to drop firebombs on the target cities—they were to be left alone.

A map of Japan showing the target cities for the atomic bomb.

HOKKAIDO

N

Niigata

HONSHU   Tokyo

Kyoto

Hiroshima

Kokura

Nagasaki

SHIKOKU

KYUSHU

0   200 miles

0   300 km

✵ Atomic bomb explosion

● Potential bomb target

■ Capital city

Hiroshima Is Bombed

On the afternoon of August 5, 1945, President Truman gave the order to drop the atomic bomb on the city of Hiroshima. Hours later, at 2:45 A.M. on

August 6, a B-29 bomber took off from an American airfield on the Pacific island of Tinian, 1,700 miles (2,740 km) from its target. On board the plane, flown by Colonel Paul W. Tibbets, was the Little Boy atomic bomb. Flying behind the bomber were two observation planes, carrying cameras and scientific instruments.

For some weeks before Hiroshima was bombed, an American weather plane had flown high over the city. The city's residents had gotten used to hearing the air-raid sirens sound

Colonel Paul W. Tibbets stands beside his plane, the **Enola Gay,** *which was named after his mother.*

each day and to seeing the lone plane circling above them. When the sirens sounded at 7:00 A.M. on the

Crewmen of the **Enola Gay** *load the Little Boy atomic bomb onto the plane on the evening before it was dropped.*

morning of August 6, the weather plane could be seen as usual. There did not seem to be any cause for alarm.

The *Enola Gay* reached Hiroshima at 7:30 A.M. The weather was good, and the American bomber circled in the bright, cloudless sky at a height of around 31,000 feet (9,500 m) above the city.

At 8:15 A.M., Little Boy was dropped on Hiroshima. The aiming point was the Aioi Bridge in the center. No warning had been given to the 350,000 inhabitants. To them, it was an ordinary Monday morning, the beginning of a new week. They could have had no idea what one 10-foot-long (3 m) bomb was going to do to their city.

Death of a City and Its Peopl

As soon as the *Enola Gay* had released Little Boy, the plane turned and flew from the scene. It took about a minute for Little Boy to fall by parachute to the point at which it exploded. It was not designed to hit the ground. Instead, it blew up at 1,900 feet (580 m) above Hiroshima. It had the same force as 13,750 tons (12,500 t) of conventional explosives.

Inside the *Enola Gay*, bright light from the explosion filled the plane. Colonel Tibbets and his crew turned to look back at Hiroshima. They wore Polaroid goggles to protect their eyes from the blinding flash of light. Tibbets said: *"The city was hidden by that awful cloud . . . boiling up, mushrooming."* Captain Robert Lewis, the copilot, said: *"My God, what have we done?"*

The mushroom cloud from the atomic explosion rising into the sky above the city of Hiroshima.

No one knows exactly how many people died as a result of the atomic explosion at Hiroshima on August 6, 1945. Most estimates say that 70,000 people died instantly—from the heat and the blast. The explosion caused a wind that blew at 1,444 feet (440 m) per second, and the temperature reached 9,000°F (5,000°C).

More deadly still was the effect of radiation—an invisible force released by the bomb that entered people's bodies and caused them to die days, weeks, months, and years after the bombing. In 1946, a report put the civilian death toll at 118,661. Some estimates say the present death toll is as high as 200,000.

As for Hiroshima itself, 90 percent of the city's buildings were destroyed.

A bleak view of the city of Hiroshima after the bombing.

Nagasaki Is Bombed

Three days after the bombing of Hiroshima, Nagasaki suffered the same fate. A B-29 bomber, nicknamed *Bockscar,* piloted by Major Charles W. Sweeney, set off for the city of Kokura, carrying the Fat Man atomic bomb. But Kokura was hidden by cloud, so the plane was diverted to Nagasaki.

Fat Man fell by parachute. At 11:02 on the morning of August 9, 1945, it exploded 1,640 feet (500 m) above the ground. It had the same force as 24,200 tons (22,000 t) of ordinary explosives. About 270,000 people lived in Nagasaki and an estimated 75,000 died. In the years that followed, the death toll increased to 150,000. One-third of the city was destroyed.

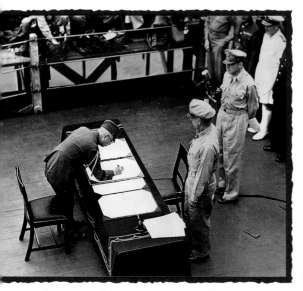

Japanese delegates sign the official documents of surrender.

The day before the bombing, the Soviet Union declared war on Japan. Faced with this, and with the U.S. using its super-bomb, Japan surrendered on August 14. The Second World War was over, and the atomic bomb had changed the world forever.

Postscript

Was it necessary to use the atomic bomb? Even after all this time, opinions are divided between those for it and those against it.

President Truman, the politician who gave the order to drop the bomb, said: *"This is the greatest thing in history."* Leo Szilard, the scientist who worked on the bomb, said: *"Using atomic bombs against Japan is one of the greatest blunders of history."* Albert Einstein, whose letter encouraged the U.S. to build the bomb, said: *"I could burn my fingers that I wrote that first letter to Roosevelt."*

Sankichi Toge wrote this famous poem. He died in 1953, from leukemia caused by radiation. He was a victim of the Hiroshima bomb.

Give Back the Human
Give back my father, give back my mother;
Give back my elders;
Give me my sons and daughters back.
Give me back myself,
Give back the human race.
As long as this life lasts, this life,
Give back peace
That will never end.

Timeline

1938   Otto Hahn and Fritz Strassmann of Germany split the uranium atom.

1939   *August 2:* Albert Einstein writes to President Roosevelt with news about the potential for building a bomb with uranium.

1939   *September 3:* The Second World War begins.

1939   *October 19:* President Roosevelt replies to Einstein.

1941   *October 9:* President Roosevelt decides that the United States should build an atomic bomb.

1941   *December 6:* The Manhattan Project begins, with the aim of building the United States' atomic bomb.

1941   *December 7:* America enters the war after Japan attacks the U.S. naval base at Pearl Harbor, Hawaii.

1942   *November 16:* Los Alamos, New Mexico, is chosen as the place for the atomic bomb laboratory.

1945   *April 12:* President Roosevelt dies. Harry S. Truman becomes the new president of the United States.

1945   *May 8:* Germany surrenders. War in Europe ends.

1945   *July 16:* First atomic device is successfully tested, at Alamogordo, New Mexico (Trinity Test).

1945   *July 17:* The Potsdam Conference begins.

1945   *July 21:* President Truman approves an order for atomic bombs to be used.

1945	*July 25:* U.S. Air Force is given written instructions for the bombing of cities in Japan.
1945	*July 26:* Japan is told to surrender.
1945	*July 28:* Japan refuses to surrender.
1945	*August 2:* The Potsdam Conference ends.
1945	*August 6:* An atomic bomb is dropped on Hiroshima.
1945	*August 8:* The Soviet Union declares war on Japan.
1945	*August 9:* An atomic bomb is dropped on Nagasaki.
1945	*August 14:* Japan surrenders. The Second World War ends.
1945	*September 2:* Japan signs the surrender documents.

The A-Bomb Dome, Hiroshima, as it is today. The atomic bomb exploded above it.

Glossary

atomic bomb An explosive device in which a great amount of energy is released in a very short space of time.

chain reaction A process in which one reaction causes another reaction to occur, which, in turn, produces a further reaction, and so on. The reactions are all linked together.

conventional bombs Devices that use "ordinary" explosives, of which there are many types.

plutonium A silvery-white metallic substance used in the making of the atomic bomb. It is man-made and does not occur in nature.

split the atom A process in which atoms are made to release energy in a chain reaction, leading to an atomic explosion.

uranium A silvery-white metallic substance found in nature which was used in the making of the atomic bomb.

Who's Who?

Sir Winston Churchill British Prime Minister from 1940 to 1945, and from 1951 to 1955.

Albert Einstein German-born, Nobel Prize-winning Jewish scientist. In the 1930s he fled to the U.S., becoming a U.S. citizen in 1940.

General Leslie R. Groves American head of the Manhattan Project from 1942 until 1947.

Dr. Robert Oppenheimer American physicist and director of the Los Alamos laboratory.

Franklin D. Roosevelt The 32nd President of the U.S. Under him America began to build the atomic bomb.

Josef Stalin Head of state of the Soviet Union during the Second World War.

Harry S. Truman The 33rd President of the U.S. He gave the order to use the atomic bomb against Japan.

Index